SHIPS

Franklin Watts
95 Madison Avenue
New York, NY 10016

Library of Congress Cataloging-in-Publication Data

Richardson, Joy.
    Ships / by Joy Richardson.
        p. cm. – (Picture science)
    Includes index.
    ISBN 0-531-14326-0
    1.Ships–Juvenile literature. [1. Ships.] I. Title.
    II. Series: Richardson, Joy. Picture science.
    VM150.R48 1994
    623.8'2–dc20   93-49730
                                                       CIP AC

10 9 8 7 6 5 4 3 2 1

Editor: Belinda Weber
Designer: Janet Watson
Picture researcher: Sarah Moule
Illustrators: Robert and Rhoda Burns

Photographs: Chris Fairclough Colour Library 11, 18,
© Jonathan Smith 6; Eye Ubiquitous © A Cudbertson 12;
Picturepoint 15; Robert Harding Picture Library 21,
© Philip Craven 16; Tony Stone Worldwide 26, © Jean
Pragen cover, © Alastair Black 9, © Ambrose Greenway 24,
© James Andrew Boreham 28; ZEFA 23.

Printed in Malaysia

SHIPS

Joy Richardson

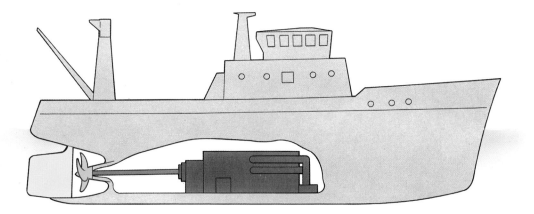

FRANKLIN WATTS

New York • Chicago • London • Toronto • Sydney

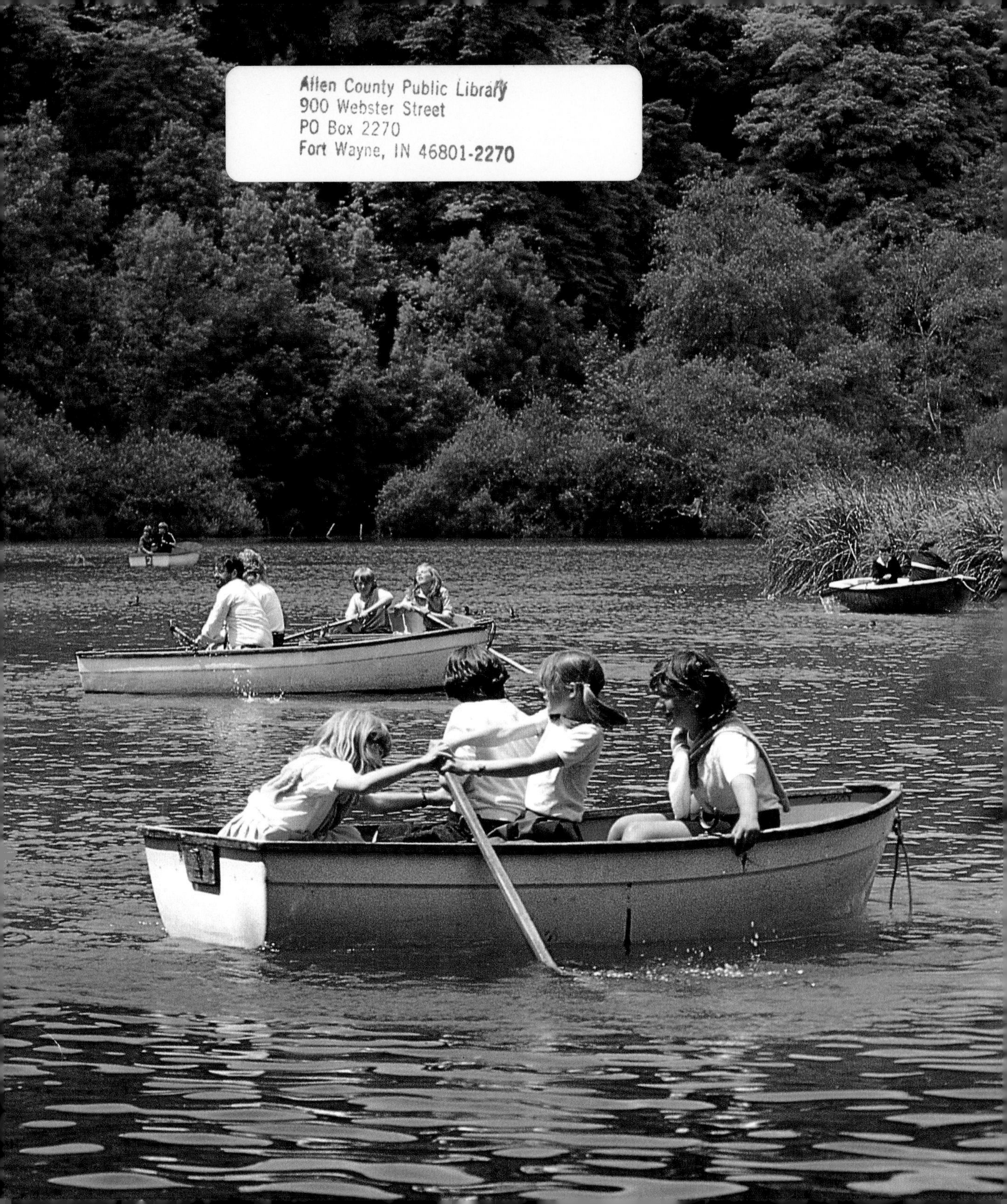

Row, row, row the boat

Long, long ago, people found
that logs could float on water.
They began to make boats
from wood and animal skins.
They used wooden paddles to
move their boats along.

The Greeks and Romans
had wooden fighting ships
rowed by hundreds of slaves.

Rowing is hard work.
It takes a lot of muscle power
to push against the water.

Wind in the sails

Sails catch the wind and use its
strength to move the ship along.

Sails are swung around
to make use of the wind
whichever way it is blowing.

Explorers and traders circled
the world in sailing ships.
The biggest ships had
at least three tall masts with
lots of sails attached to them.

Today, ships with sails
still race across the oceans.

Engine power

For the last hundred years,
most ships have had engines.
The first engines used coal to make
steam power. Now ships use fuel oil.

The engine drives propellers at the
back of the ship. The blades screw into
the water and push the ship forward.
Engine power is also needed to
make electricity for the ship.

Big ships have a large engine
room on the bottom deck.

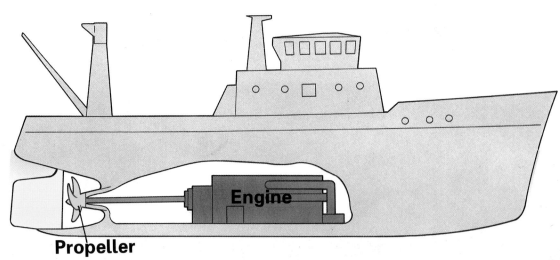

Engine

Propeller

10

A metal body

The ship's body is called the hull.

Modern ships have metal hulls.
Steel plates are welded together
to make them watertight.

The hull is shaped to keep
the ship steady in the water.

The rudder at the back moves
to change the ship's direction.
It is hidden beneath the waterline.

When the hull needs cleaning,
painting, and repairing,
the ship is taken into dry dock.

Ferry ride

Ferries carry people and cars
across short stretches of water.

Roll-on roll-off ferries have
a big door at each end.

Cars drive in one end of the
ferry and out of the other
when the ship docks.

Water slows ships down.
Hydrofoils and hovercrafts
go faster than other ferries,
because they can lift up
and skim over the surface.

Carrying cargo

Cargo ships carry goods
to ports in other countries.

Cars and computers,
food and furniture,
clothes and chemicals
all travel by cargo ship.

Cranes load metal boxes all the same
size onto huge container ships.
Refrigerated containers keep food cold.

The biggest ships in the world
are giant oil tankers more than
1,500 feet (457 m) long.

Fish factory

Fishing ships catch and
carry food from the sea.

The crew winds the net in
from the sea and onto the deck.

Fish from the net pour down through
a hatch onto a conveyor belt below.
This conveyor takes them to be
gutted, cleaned, frozen and then
stored in the hold.

While the ship is empty, tanks of
water keep the ship weighted down.
As the ship fills up with fish,
the water is pumped out.

Pleasure cruise

Cruise liners carry passengers who want to vacation on the water.

These liners are like floating hotels with bedrooms, bathrooms, kitchens, and dining rooms.

There are lots of portholes in rooms so that passengers can see out and decks with swimming pools and tennis courts.

Lots of crew members are needed to sail the ship and to take care of all the passengers.

Warships

Warships carry weapons
and keep track of the enemy.

The biggest warships are
aircraft carriers, which can carry
thousands of people ready for action.
Planes and helicopters take off
and land on the enormous deck.

Submarines can hide from sight
underwater. Water is pumped into
tanks to make the submarine sink.
When the water is pumped out, the
submarine surfaces again.

To the rescue

The sea can be dangerous.

Lifeboats rush out to rescue
people from ships that
have run into trouble.

The lifeboat can be launched quickly.
It has powerful engines and can
keep afloat in the roughest seas.

Ships carry their own life preservers
and life rafts for use in an emergency.

On the bridge

The captain is in charge of the ship,
but everyone on board has a job to do.

Radio operators work the
radio and radar systems.
Engineers run the engines.
Navigators work out the ship's route.

The ship is steered from the bridge,
a high room with a good view of the sea.
Instruments on the bridge
give information and show
the position of other ships.

Computers can now be used
to control the ship's movements.

Ship facts

The oldest surviving "ship"
is a 6,000-year-old dugout
tree trunk found in Europe.

The fastest boat was a
jet-propelled speedboat that
reached a speed of over 319 miles
per hour (513 km/h).

Wind is the cheapest power.
Big, new ships have been designed
with computer-controlled sails,
as well as engines, to save fuel.

Index